ITALY
AND
SWITZERLAND

Cultures and Costumes Series:

- The British Isles
- Oceania
- Africa
- The Middle East
- China and Japan
- Native America
- Greece and Turkey
- France
- Spain and Portugal
- Northern Europe
- Italy and Switzerland
- Eastern Europe
- India and Sri Lanka

ITALY
AND
SWITZERLAND

PAULA HAMMOND

MASON CREST PUBLISHERS

www.masoncrest.com

Mason Crest Publishers Inc.
370 Reed Road
Broomall, PA 19008
(866) MCP-BOOK (toll free)
www.masoncrest.com

First printing 2002

1 2 3 4 5 6 7 8 9 10

Library of Congress Cataloging-in-Publication Data available

ISBN 1-59084-438-6

Printed and bound in Malaysia

Editorial and design by
Amber Books Ltd.
Bradley's Close
74–77 White Lion Street
London N1 9PF

Project Editor: Marie-Claire Muir
Designer: Hawes Design
Picture Research: Lisa Wren

Picture Credits:
All pictures courtesy of Amber Books Ltd, except the following:
Popperfoto: 10.

ACKNOWLEDGMENT
For authenticating this book, the Publishers would like to thank
Robert L. Humphrey, Jr., Professor Emeritus of Anthropology,
George Washington University, Washington, D.C.

Contents

Switzerland

Italy

Situated in southern
Europe and shaped
like a boot, much of
Italy is mountainous.
The snowy peaks
of the Alps cross
northern Italy and
fill most of southern
Switzerland.

Introduction

Nearly every species in the animal kingdom adapts to changes in the environment. To cope with cold weather, the cat adapts by growing a longer coat of fur, the bear hibernates, and birds migrate to a different climatic zone. Only humans use costume and culture—what they have learned through many generations—to adapt to the environment.

The first humans developed their culture by using spears to hunt the bear, knives and scrapers to skin it, and needles and sinew to turn the hide into a warm coat to insulate their hairless bodies. As time went on, the clothes humans wore became an indicator of cultural and individual differences. Some were clearly developed to be more comfortable in the environment, others were designed for decorative, economic, political, and religious reasons.

Ritual costumes can tell us about the deities, ancestors, and civil and military ranking in a society, while other clothing styles can identify local or national identity. Social class, gender, age, economic status, climate, profession, and political persuasion are also reflected in clothing. Anthropologists have even tied changes in the hemline length of women's dresses to periods of cultural stress or relative calm.

In 13 beautifully illustrated volumes, the *Cultures and Costumes: Symbols of their Period* series explores the remarkable variety of costumes found around the world and through different eras. Each book shows how different societies have clothed themselves, revealing a wealth of diverse and sometimes mystifying explanations. Costume can be used as a social indicator by scientists, artists, cinematographers, historians, and designers—and also provide students with a better understanding of their own and other cultures.

ROBERT L. HUMPHREY, JR., Professor Emeritus of Anthropology,
George Washington University, Washington, D.C.

Ancient Rome and the Etruscans

The glory that was Rome did not develop overnight, nor did it spring fully formed out of the soil beside the Tiber. The style that became identified with Rome owed much to the ideas and ideals of those who came before it.

The legend of the founding of Rome is one that the people of Ancient Rome loved to retell. According to the legend, King Amulius was afraid. Since he had seized the throne of Alba Longa from his brother Numitor, he had lived in dread of a rival taking his crown. To safeguard his position, Amulius had his brother's sons brutally murdered. They, at least, would never take his crown. His niece, Rhea Silvia, could not rule in her own right, but any children she might have could rightfully claim the throne. Amulius decided that Rhea

Beauty, simplicity, and elegance were a typical feature of Roman art, architecture, and costume. Just as the toga came to symbolize ancient Roman costume, high, ornamental arches and marble columns were typical features of Roman architecture.

should become a vestal virgin. As a priestess of Vesta, the goddess of the hearth and home, Rhea's life was safe as long as she remained a virgin. Priestesses who broke this rule were buried alive.

One day, as Rhea tended the goddess' sacred flame, she was visited by Mars, the god of war, who seduced her. After nine months, Rhea gave birth to two twin boys. Furious, Amulius had his niece executed. He ordered the babies be placed in a basket and thrown into the fast-flowing waters of the Tiber River—to die.

But the babies, Romulus and Remus, survived by suckling a she-wolf and, after many years, returned to Alba Longa to kill Amulius and restore King Numitor to the throne. They then set off to found a nation of their own. After they reached a city built on seven hills, a furious argument erupted between the

Chariot racing was one of ancient Rome's most popular spectator sports. Charioteers rode for one of four main teams—the Greens, Blues, Whites, or Reds. During races, competitors and their supporters wore team colors, just as modern sports fans sometimes do today.

two brothers. In a blind rage, Romulus murdered Remus and claimed the city for himself. Rome, Romulus' city—founded on a legacy of blood and betrayal—was born.

Beginnings

Rome, the capital of modern-day Italy, has been called "the Eternal City." Nestled in the center of the narrow, boot-shaped Italian peninsula, Rome has been the focus of civilization in Western Europe for almost 1,000 years.

The first settlers arrived in Rome around 1000 B.C. During this time, Rome was part of a region called Latinum, which included much of what would become Italy. The word "Italy" comes from the Latin word for "grazing land," a name given to the region by the ancient Romans. About 800 B.C., the Etruscans, an energetic and vigorous people, moved into the region and conquered the Latin people. Today, little is known about the Etruscans. Even their language has never been deciphered. According to Roman historians, writing centuries later, the Etruscans were a cruel, barbaric people whose culture was "stolen" from civilizations more advanced than their own. However, Roman historians had little love of their old Etruscan "masters," and we cannot tell for sure how much of what they tell us is true.

We do know that the Etruscans had a rich, artistic civilization. Etruscan women, unlike most women in the ancient world, enjoyed lives of relative freedom and equality. Tombs have been discovered whose **frescoes** show both men and women taking part in sports, playing music, and enjoying banquets. They also show a love of fine living, comfort, costume, and ornamentation.

Something Borrowed...

Costume and ornamentation give a unique insight into a culture's ideals and beliefs. Etruscan dress, shown in sculptures and frescoes, is similar to the clothing of other cultures in the region, apparently supporting the Roman claim that the Etruscans were cultural "thieves." In reality, however, this did not mean that Etruscan culture lacked creativity. The Romans themselves were greatly influenced by ancient Greece, and freely adopted what they liked from Greek art, literature, philosophy, and costume. The Etruscans, too, looked toward ancient Greece for cultural guidance and inspiration.

Mycenaean and Minoan costume was famed for its rich colors, ornamentation, and jewelry. Later, the ancient Greeks preferred simpler, more elegant styles. Etruscan dress was bright and richly decorated, blending the tailored look of late Minoan and Mycenaean clothing with the long, draped costumes worn by the ancient Greeks—not so much "cultural theft" as a blending of ideas to create something new that the Etruscans could call their own.

Men and Women

Italy has been called "the sunny country" because of its warm, humid climate. Although we cannot be sure, it is likely that Etruscan clothes were made from

A Win-Win Situation

The ancient Romans loved sports and held regular chariot races at a huge stadium called the Circus Maximus. According to legend, Romulus organized the first chariot race, but the first real stadium was probably designed by the Etruscans. Wearing leather helmets and chest armor for protection, charioteers were dressed in red, green, white, or blue to show which team they rode for. Nero, an emperor in the first century A.D., was a fanatical fan of these games and always wore green at the Circus to show support for his favorite team. Nero's love of sports stemmed from his own supposed athletic **prowess**. While in Greece, Nero competed at the Olympic Games. Despite falling from his chariot and failing to finish the race, he was still awarded the victor's crown of olive leaves.

either wool or linen, depending on the materials available locally. Linen is made from the fibers of the flax plant, which has been used to make clothes for at least 10,000 years. Egyptian **mummies** were wrapped in linen, and both the Greeks and ancient Hebrews wore it. Linen is an ideal material for warm Mediterranean climates, as it is both strong and lightweight. Wool, too, when woven finely, can be soft and cool. Such fine cloth can be draped easily over the body and, when worn in layers, drops naturally into soft, flattering folds.

Etruscan dress for men looked a little like a Greek *chiton*, which was a knee- or calf-length tunic pinned in place at the shoulders. Some paintings from the period also show men in waist-length tunics and tailored shorts, which may have been worn for athletic contests. Cloaks were worn in many styles, again showing the influence of other cultures. The two most common were a long, woolen cloak, which looked like a Greek garment called a *himation*, and a flowing cape with wide sleeves, which resembled a Persian *kandy*.

For women, clothes were worn long and generally sewn to the shape of the body. These gowns usually had elbow-length sleeves that flared out at the ends. Bright colors and hems, cuffs, and necklines decorated with geometric shapes combined to give the finished effect.

Etruscan shoes and ankle boots also came in bright colors. These were made from natural plant dyes, which produced rich reds, browns, and greens. Made from cloth or leather, both styles generally had toes that curled up at the ends. Knee-length boots and, later, sandals were also worn.

In addition to a Greek-style tunic, Etruscan men also wore longer, sleeved tunics that were tied at the waist, as shown.

Etruscans preferred to be bare-headed. When the weather was bad, a conical shaped hat with a rolled brim was worn by both men and women.

Gold, Bronze, and Glass

The Etruscans' greatest artistic achievements can be seen in their spectacular jewelry. Etruscans used a process called granulation, in which gold powder is scattered on a metallic base to make intricate patterns. They were also experts in filigree and enameling. Filigree uses strips of metallic wire to make extremely delicate ornamentation in a process that requires enormous skill and patience. Enameling is an equally demanding process involving heating ground and colored glass to high temperatures. The resulting liquid is then poured onto a prepared metallic surface to produce a design that is inlaid into the metal.

Bronze was also used to make earrings, bracelets, and necklaces. Baule earrings were a particularly popular style worn by the Etruscans. Baule means "barrel" or "case"—the earrings were made from strips of gold or bronze folded into a cylindrical shape.

Despite what the Romans may have said, the beauty of such jewelry shows the true richness of Etruscan culture—a culture from which an independent Roman republic eventually emerged during the fifth century B.C.

Bring on the Romans

Roman history is divided into three periods: the kingdom, the republic, and the empire. Under the rule of the Etruscan kings, Rome and the surrounding regions became rich and powerful. Finally, in 509 B.C., Rome had grown strong enough to overthrow her Etruscan ruler—the impressively named Tarquinius

Superbus. Over the next 500 years, from 509 to 27 B.C., the republic of Rome became the dominant power in the region, gobbling up the remainder of the Etruscan empire, conquering the **Gauls** and **Samnites**, and extending its control into Africa and Spain by the end of the **Punic Wars** (264–146 B.C.).

After a period of instability in which a series of dictators wrestled for control of the republic, Augustus pronounced himself Rome's first emperor in 27 B.C. Although by this time Rome was already at the center of a huge territory, it only became a true empire under Augustus. This is because *empire* is a political term used to describe rule by one person—an emperor. For the next 200 years, the Roman Empire continued to expand its power and influence, dominating thought, culture, and costume throughout the ancient world. Yet the key features of Roman civilization were not uniquely Roman. Just as the Etruscans had borrowed from the Greeks, so, too, did the Romans. After the conquest of Greece in 146 B.C., Greek ideas on art, literature, and clothing flowed into the empire. So strong was this process of **Hellenization** that the Roman writer Cicero asked sadly: "What remains of the old ways in which…the Roman states stood rooted?"

Gift-Giving

The Latin poet Martial wrote a series of gift tags in the form of single-**couplet** poems. These were designed to be used with gifts given at the Saturnalia festival, which took place in December each year. These tags show the humorous side of Roman gift-giving. One, designed as a tag for a *mamillare*, which was a length of cloth women wore around their breasts, reads: "Compress the swelling breasts of my mistress that there may be something for my hand to cover and seize." Another, for a *strigil* (a knife used to clean off sweat and dirt), read: "Scrape yourself with the curved blade: then the laundryman will not often wear out your towels."

Togas and Tunics

When we think of ancient Rome, we think of the **toga**. Roman people loved beauty and elegance, but also valued practical ideas and hard work. The toga represents the Roman mind better than any sculpture or fresco. This one costume is both elegant and practical: a simple design that appealed to the Roman character. The Romans were also unique in the ancient world in that they had a strong sense of their own place in history. They talked of how future generations would see them, and loved tradition and ritual. Part of this tradition included wearing togas. To the Romans, as the centuries progressed, the toga became more and more a symbolic costume—something that represented Roman history and ideals rather than just an everyday garment.

Especially during the period of the republic, togas were the standard item of clothing for citizens (center and right). The emperor (center) wears a laurel wreath on his head. The lictor (left) bears the emperor's insignia.

Someone Has to Do It

Being a fuller was one of the most unpleasant trades in ancient Rome. Fullers cleaned and maintained clothing. This was a dirty, smelly, and hazardous job. Cloth for cleaning went through many processes in which the material was bleached, combed, and softened. Bleaching was particularly unpleasant, as the clothes had to be hung over a pit of smoldering sulfur that burned the fuller's lungs and stung his eyes. The **nap** of the cloth would then be combed by rubbing it with hedgehog skins, which chaffed and cut the fuller's hands. Finally, urine, collected daily from the public toilets, would be trod and kneaded into the material to thicken and soften the cloth. No wonder this was a process that most Romans preferred not to do at home.

The toga was based on the Greek *himation*. A *himation* was a long woolen cloak worn draped around the body to protect the wearer from the cold and rain. The process of draping the toga was complex, and a range of styles developed to suit the preferences of the wearer. Togas could also be troublesome. A typical toga was made from heavy woolen cloth, generally 18 feet long by 5 feet wide (almost 5.5 m by 1.7 m wide). Putting on a toga was at least a two-person job—and keeping it correctly pinned, layered, and draped was equally tricky.

Not surprisingly, by the second century A.D., the wearing of togas had declined among the general population, although it continued to be worn by Roman officials and by ordinary citizens during festivals and celebrations. In its place, the *pallium*, which was smaller and easier to wear, soon became a popular outdoor costume for men. For indoors, a **tunica**, which was almost identical to the Greek *chiton*, was worn. By the third century, a further adaptation in costume occurred with the addition of a long, ankle-length *tunica* over the shorter version.

What Lies Beneath

Togas were initially worn over a loincloth. By the time of the Roman Empire, only the poor still wore this early form of underwear. Richer Romans preferred knee-length trousers, called *femoralia*, which were worn beneath the toga. As the Roman writer Horace discovered to his embarrassment, a toga that was incorrectly draped would reveal the underwear below. For such a *faux pas*, Horace was laughed at in the street, an incident that distressed him so much that he recorded his shame for **posterity**.

For women, the basic Roman costume was the *stola*. This was a long, flowing garment generally gathered under the breast or at the waist with a **girdle**. *Stolas* were worn with sleeves—which were sewn or pinned in place—or without. The female equivalent of the toga was the *palla*, which was also based on a Greek style. A head scarf completed the costume.

Rules and Regulations

The wearing of togas was strictly regulated by law as well as custom. Only citizens of Rome could wear a toga, and the color of a toga was used to show the wearer's social status. A white *toga pura* was worn by tribunes, who were elected officials. Magistrates wore a *toga praetexta*, which had a purple stripe along the edge of the cloth. Only the emperor could wear a toga of pure purple. In much of the ancient world, royal or **Tyrian purple** could be worn only by the ruling elite. This was because the rich bluish-red dye was difficult and expensive to manufacture. Over time, anything associated with this color came to be thought of as special, which is why, even today, ceremonial robes and carpets are red.

The same rules applied to *tunicas*. The ruling class wore white, probably because only those who did not have to work for a living could wear it all day without getting it dirty. Ordinary citizens wore brown or undyed *tunicas*.

Roman costume followed ancient Greek styles, shown here, using lengths of finely woven linen or wool, which were draped around the body to create simple but stylish garments.

Length, cut, and quality of costume were all important. Rich women wore long *stolas* with a train at the back. Quality material was expensive, and a long gown was an indication of wealth. Tacitus, a Roman historian, outlined the basic rules for togas: "The front edge of the tunic should come a little below the knee; in the back, to the middle of the knees. For below this point, it is the dress of a woman; above, that of a **centurion**." Cloaks, too, came in a variety of styles that denoted the wearer's rank. Soldiers wore the *paludamentum* and *sagum*, officers the longer, heavier *paludamentum*, and the rank and file wore the shorter *sagum*.

These designs, from 18th-century Bologna, show the enduring legacy of Rome in styles of decoration and ornamentation. Notice the statues of Roman soldiers in leather skirts and iron helmets.

The Cut of the Cloth

Despite the slow Hellenization complained of by Cicero, by the time of the Empire, Roman costume had become much richer and more ornate than the Greek styles they tried to copy. While the Greeks believed that simplicity in dress equalled elegance, the Roman elite enjoyed displaying their wealth.

Linen and wool remained the fabrics of choice for many, but gradually cotton, imported from India, became a favorite with the wealthy. Silk, too, although expensive, was in great demand and was imported into the Empire in vast quantities from China.

For women especially, ornamentation became increasingly spectacular. Rich dyes were used to produce costumes of dazzling shades of yellow, blue, red, and green. Pleats and fringes were added to *stolas*, and richly embroidered girdles and jewelry gave an added feeling of **opulence**.

Unlike the Greeks, wealthy Romans liked to change their clothes regularly throughout the day. Layers of *tunicas* were also worn, one on top of the other, especially toward the fourth century A.D. This increase in the size of the average Roman's wardrobe reflected the Empire's growing prosperity. By the end of the Empire, clothing that had traditionally been made in the home could be bought ready-made in shops called *tabernae*. In the rest of the Empire, too, the demand for more and richer clothing grew. While only Roman citizens could legally wear togas, this did not stop wealthy imitators in the provinces from copying Roman costume. For centuries after the fall of the Roman Empire, Western Europe would continue copying Roman art, costume, and architecture in an attempt to recapture some of the glory that was Rome.

Too Much, Too Little

Hair styling was an integral part of Roman costume. During the Roman republic, women's hair was generally worn tied back, but by the time of the Empire, styles could be ridiculously extravagant. Juvenal, a Roman **satirist**, mocked these fashions, saying: "See the tall edifice rise up on her head…the effect is ultra-absurd."

However, having hair to style was considered better than having none at all. Roman men worried constantly about losing their hair and went to great lengths to preserve their thinning locks. Rat droppings were a favorite home remedy. In contrast, Roman women had to worry about too much hair. Facial hair was seen as undesirable and had to be scrubbed off with a **pumice stone** or pulled out using a mix of pitch and resin that was applied to the skin. This was then painfully peeled off, pulling the unwanted hair out by its roots—an early form of waxing.

The Italian City-States

During the Middle Ages, Italian city-states grew in wealth, power, and independence. Not only did Italy's citizens look different from each other, their costumes were also recognizably different from those worn in the rest of Europe.

The destruction of the Roman Empire did not happen overnight, with a spectacular natural disaster or a devastating war. Rather, the Empire was chipped away slowly, over many centuries, by a combination of invaders, disease, and poor government.

In A.D. 395, Roman territories were officially split into two separate empires—the eastern, which eventually became the Byzantine empire, and the Western, which remained under the control of Rome. Gradually, while this new eastern empire grew in strength, the Western empire crumbled further. Finally, in A.D. 476, the Germanic chieftain Odoacer marched his clansmen

These representations of 16th-century European costume show the difference between Italian fashions (top row), English styles (bottom row), and a French costume (bottom row, far left). Italian ladies displayed their wealth by wearing greater volumes and more elaborately decorated cloth than their European counterparts.

An Amazing Feet

Long-toed shoes, called *poulaines*, were popular in Italy during the 1350s. The style soon spread to the rest of Europe. By 1380, some shoes had toe-points up to two feet long (60 cm). To keep their shape, these points were packed with wadding or stiffened with whalebone. This made walking virtually impossible, and a chain was sometimes fastened to the tip of the shoe and around the knee to keep the toe-point out of the way.

into Rome and forced Emperor Romulus Augustulus from the throne.

The fall of Rome shook Europe to its core, throwing it into a Dark Age that lasted almost 500 years.

The Rise of the City-States

During the Dark Ages, four centers of power emerged in Europe: the Carolingian empire, the Byzantine empire, the Arab empire, and the **Papacy**. The Carolingian empire, under Charlemagne (A.D. 771–814), dominated most of what is modern-day France and Germany. In Spain and North Africa, the main cultural

The marriage of Boccaccio Adimari to Lisa Ricasoli took place in Florence in 1420. The bride (on p 24) wears a richly embroidered black velvet gown. The groom, beside her, is the only adult male who is bareheaded.

influences were Arabian. Byzantium ruled most of Greece, Turkey, and Eastern Europe.

In Rome and the surrounding Italian cities, it was the Papacy that had much of the power—although, initially, from behind the scenes. After periods of rule by Odoacer, the Ostrogoths, and a short period back under the control of "old Rome" in the form of the Byzantine empire, Italy came under the control of another Germanic tribe, the Lombards. But through all this, one force remained consistent—the Papacy.

In Christian theology, Saint Peter, the first Pope, was given authority by Jesus Christ to represent God's will on earth. The Pope became the leader of the Christian Church and supreme head of the Church's system of government, called the Papacy. It was Pope Gregory I (A.D. 590–640) who first extended the Church's influence beyond faith and into politics. By instituting taxes throughout Italy, he raised enough money to feed the population and pay an army. By A.D. 774, the Papacy, aided by Charlemagne, King of the Franks (A.D. 771–814), was finally able to crush the Lombards and establish papal rule in central Italy. As thanks for his help, Pope Leo III crowned Charlemagne king of Rome in A.D. 800. This was the beginning of a period of stability that saw the foundation of a Europe-wide Holy Roman Empire.

With stability came prosperity. By the 1300s, Italian cities, which were ideally placed on the trade routes from Europe to the east, were wealthy and powerful. Florence, Milan, Venice, Pisa, and Genoa were just some of these new, independent city-states that had grown rich on trade.

Many Cities, Many Styles

During the 14th and 15th centuries, national rather than regional styles of dress appeared in Europe. Under strong leaders, places such as England developed a concept of nationhood in which the population shared a common language, culture, and mode of dress. In Italy's city-states, an "Italian" identity that could be expressed through costume did not develop until many centuries later. The Italian city-states were founded on trade and remained fiercely independent and competitive with each other. It was only after centuries of foreign domination of the region that people like Guiseppe Mazzini, an Italian patriot, realized that strength lay in unity. Italy's city-states were finally united as one nation in 1861 under King Victor Emmanuel II. Italy would not become a republic until 1947.

During these early centuries, however, unity was a long way off and fashions not only varied from those in the rest of Europe, but also among city-states. A fashionable Venetian man of the 1400s, for example, could be identified by the fact that the **hose** he wore on his left leg was patterned. In Florence, a hat called a *berretino* identified the wearer as a foreigner, as Florentine men preferred to wear plumed hats called *toques*. This competitiveness also meant that fashions in the city-states changed more quickly than in the rest of Europe. Each city wanted to be the first to adopt a new style, and because of this, Italian fashion led the world for almost 300 years.

Funeral Crafts and Love Nests

Venice is built on a series of islands next to the Italian coast. Instead of streets, it has canals, and even today, one of the most popular ways of traveling on these is by gondola. A gondola is a narrow boat propelled by a gondolier, who pushes the vessel along with a pole. Traditionally, gondolas were decorated in vivid hues and draped with fine fabrics. This was intended to display the wealth of the noble family that owned it. Gondoliers, too, dressed in expensive and exotic uniforms. To stop this costly and wasteful rivalry, various laws were brought in, and eventually all gondolas had to be black. The sight of these funeral-black crafts slipping, almost soundlessly, through the canals made the German writer Thomas Mann compare the gondola to a coffin bound on a last, silent journey. Despite this eerie image, lovers often used gondolas. The addition of a black cloth, draped over wooden hoops, turned the gondola into an ideal private meeting place. Because of this, gondoliers got a bad reputation. Thomas Coryat, an English traveler, commented in 1595 that gondoliers were "the most vicious and **licentious** varlets about the city."

Tight-fitting, patterned hose and figure-hugging tunics were the usual costume for gondoliers. Two rival groups controlled public gondoliers in Venice; the Nicolotti wore dark colors and the Castellani wore reds.

Hose and Dagged Edges

For the men and women of Venice, where some of Europe's most luxurious cloth was produced, fashions of the 14th century were lavish and expensive. While regional variations abounded, most men wore three main items of clothing. These were a tight-fitting, long-sleeved shirt, a short tunic-jacket worn over the shirt, and a pair of hose. Hose were a type of woolen or silk stocking. These were made as separate legs and were originally knee-length. By the 1360s, hose were made to cover the entire leg. They were kept in place by laces, called points, which tied the top of the stocking to holes around the underside of the tunic. Attached to the tunic was a short, above-the-knee skirt in a style called a **pourpoint**. The tunic's sleeves were tight-fitting, with long streams of material—sometimes several feet long—left hanging from the wrist. This length of cloth was called a tippet.

During the early 15th century, the *houppelande*, which was a long, flowing, unisex gown with dagged edges, became popular. Dagged edges were a form of decoration in which hems and cuffs were cut into jagged shapes. *Houppelandes* were especially popular with older men who were less willing to show off their legs in hose. The *houppelande* remained a fashionable garment for many decades, although the cut of the gown changed slightly.

By the mid-15th century, a growing interest in the ideas of ancient Rome, in which the human body was admired, brought about new developments in art, architecture, and costume. These ideas soon filtered through to all sections of society, and a "rebirth" of the classical ideas of ancient Rome and Greece began. This time came to be known as the **Renaissance**.

The Renaissance

The Renaissance was born in the Italian city-states. The spectacular outpouring of art, literature, and learning that produced the sculptures of Michelangelo, the paintings of Leonardo da Vinci, and the plays and poetry of William Shakespeare began in Italy around 1350. By the 1450s, the Renaissance

A fashionable Venetian (left) wears colored hose on his left leg, and the Florentine man (right) wears a slashed tunic and plumed hat. These costumes date from the Renaissance.

had spread throughout Europe. Kings, such as England's Henry VIII, invited Italians to court and encouraged English scholars to study the works of ancient Rome. The key principle of the Renaissance was a Christian humanism, which blended religion and philosophy in an attempt to better understand mankind.

Humanists had strong ideas on how the ideal man or woman should dress and behave. A "Renaissance man" was expected to be educated in both arts and sciences, courteous, brave, and well dressed.

Despite the Church's disapproval, Renaissance clothing, especially in Italy, was designed to show off the figure. In Italy's city-states, clothes became tighter, with padding used on tunics to emphasize the body's shape. Hose were now made as one complete garment, which could be made to fit the leg tightly. These were often decorated with stripes to emphasize the length of the leg.

Codpieces, originally designed as a practical way of covering the male genitals, became more elaborate, emphasizing the wearer's masculinity. Tunics became shorter, and the pourpoint skirt disappeared entirely in Italy, allowing the wearer to show off his buttocks. Slashed sleeves, in which the tunic's sleeve was cut to reveal the shirt below, were also popular.

Italian men, unlike their European counterparts, were usually clean-shaven. In the 1300s, most men wore their hair in a neat bob. By 1420, longer, curled styles—echoing those seen in ancient Greek and Roman sculptures—were popular. Heads were left uncovered or were topped with a beret-style cap. This was in contrast to the elaborate rimmed hats popular in the rest of Europe. In all, the Italian city-states continued to set their own styles.

This image shows a selection of costumes worn by students at some of Rome's numerous religious schools during the 17th century. With the exception of the figure on the far left, most of these styles are similar to those worn by clerics today.

Butchers, Bakers, and Candlestick Makers

Clothes for wealthy Italians were made to reflect the best that the city-states had to offer: the beautiful embroideries of Sicily, Venetian **damasks** and velvets, and the fine silks of Florence and Milan. Venice, in particular, produced some of the best luxury goods in Europe, including fine leather work, jewelry, armor, and beautiful silk from workshops in the Calle della Bissa.

Nowhere were the wealth of Venice and the skills of her craftsmen better displayed than in the procession of the *arti* (the trade unions of the day) in honor of the new **Doge** in 1268. Martino de Canale, a Venetian customs clerk, described the procession in which the guild workers marched wearing examples of their work.

His description shows Venice at her most luxurious: furriers dressed in scarlet **samite** and **ermine** mantles, master tailors in white silk, cloak makers in rich, fur-lined robes, quilt makers in white cloaks decorated with delicate *fleurs-de-lis*, and jewelers wearing necklaces of gold, silver, and gems. Beside them marched the butchers in scarlet, barbers attended by servants dressed as knights, and lamp makers with live birds in their lanterns that were released at the height of the procession—a spectacular vision of an extraordinary city.

Married to the Sea

The Doge stepped aboard his ceremonial barge. Followed eagerly by a great number of small boats and gondolas, his attendants rowed him out into the

Faking It

In Venice, bereaved men wore plain black garments in place of their usual colorful costumes. Tradition demanded that the bereaved should also allow his beard to grow as a sign of grief—as only a carefree man had time for shaving. Until the 1600s, men could buy false beards, called *barba alla greca,* rather than go beardless at a funeral.

gently bobbing sea. Steadying himself on the barge, he stood and looked out across the deep, dark waters toward the glittering city of Venice. Holding out a small gold ring, which the Pope had blessed, he declared clearly and evenly, "We espouse thee, O sea," and dropped the wedding band into the waters below.

This annual celebration was part of a 15-day festival commemorating Doge Pietro Orseolo II's rescue of the country of Dalmatia from pirate rule. The ring was a replica of one given by Pope Alexander III to another Doge, Sebastiano

Ceremonial costumes worn by the Doge of Venice during the 9th (left) and 11th centuries (center and right). Few changes in costume occurred during this period.

Lorenzo the Magnificent

Lorenzo de' Medici (1449–1492), a member of Florence's ruling family, owned 30 spectacular robes. It has been estimated that each of these cost more than an average Florentine family might spend in a year. He became known as Lorenzo the Magnificent because of his lavish lifestyle.

Ziani, in 1177. With the commemoration of both events, the power of the Doges, as Venice's rulers, was remembered and celebrated. The festival also acknowledged Venice's reliance on the sea, with the Doge, as representative of the city, symbolically marrying the waters.

Doge was a title given to the chief magistrate of Venice (and also of Genoa). The Doge was elected for life and usually chosen from one of the city's most powerful families. As the most influential man in the land, the Doge reflected the wealth and importance of the city by the clothes that he wore.

A 14th-century Doge (right) wears the official *corno ducale* hat. The 15th-century Doge (left) is dressed for battle.

A collection of 16th-century Italian women's fashions. The shields that the women lean on would have originally held the name of the region that they came from. Such images were intended to give fashionable ladies new style ideas.

In the **Middle Ages**, the Doge wore a cloak and a long cassock, which was belted at the waist and looked a little like clerical **vestments**. By the 1200s, with Venice's increasing wealth, these robes were made in Tyrian purple. For ceremonial occasions, a crown of gold and jewels, called the *corno*, replaced the Doge's everyday brimless hat, called the *corno ducale*. By 1473, Doge Nicolo Marcello's ceremonial costumes were even richer, with a cloak of gold cloth, Tyrian purple hose, and a robe edged with ermine. In 1532, more ornamentation was added so that Doge Andrea Gritti's cloak was festooned with floral patterns embroidered onto the cloth in silver thread.

Sumptuary Laws

Both the Doge and his wife, the Dogaressa, were exempt from Venice's **sumptuary laws**, which were introduced in the 13th and 14th centuries to maintain social distinctions. With so many traders and merchants in the city-states getting rich, large sections of society could now afford to dress well. Even working-class men and women were able to rent clothes or buy last year's fashions secondhand. The nobility worried that soon no one would be able to tell how important they were simply by looking at them. The immense amount of money spent on clothing also created problems for the economy.

The introduction of strict rules regarding what clothing could be worn and by whom was an attempt to curb some of the city-states' fashion excesses. Of course, this did not work. Wealthy men and women felt that ornamentation and jewels were their "insignia of worth" and either ignored or bent the rules whenever they could. Traveler and writer Fynes Moryson described how Venetian merchants of the 1600s wore their rich clothes underneath plainer outfits, which they discarded once they reached their destination. Even the threat of excommunication, which meant being excluded from the Church community, did not stop one group of women from wearing banned fabrics at a wedding in Bologna.

Rich merchants, their wives, sons, daughters, and attendants all joyfully ignored the sumptuary laws. The writer Giovanni della Casa summed up the Italian attitude to fashion in his book on **etiquette**, saying: "Everyone should dress well according to his age and position in society…If he does not, it will be taken as a mark of contempt for other people."

A Man of the People

Not all Italians liked to dress extravagantly. Public figures who wanted to be seen as champions of the people would often deliberately "dress down"— wearing simple, undecorated tunics and linen bands wrapped around their legs. Their wives would follow suit, wearing equally plain robes. Their only ornamentation would often be a necklace of small golden rings, which was traditionally worn by working-class women.

P. VERONÈSE

Noblewomen and Courtesans

Beauty is in the eye of the beholder, but for Italy's wealthy women, appearances were everything. Ladies ensured the good opinion of others by making the most of their looks, wearing sumptuous garments and expensive accessories.

The wedding celebrations had reached their peak. In the garden of the Palazzo Medici, an orchestra played a lively tune while, all around, guests dressed in rich **brocades** and silks made short work of the first of the five wedding feasts. On one table, the bride, dressed in a white and gold brocade dress, talked and smiled, entertaining her rich and influential guests. The groom, dark-haired and serious, stood apart from the celebrations, brooding silently.

The wedding of Lorenzo de' Medici, the son of Florence's ruling family, to Clarice Orsini was not the happy event that the bride and groom's families might have hoped. Lorenzo was in love with Lucrezia Donati, but his marriage to the daughter of a wealthy Roman family had been arranged by his parents as a way of uniting these two powerful families.

This image, based on a painting by the artist Veronese (1528–1588), shows Venetian noblewomen at the end of the 16th century dressed in heavily embroidered velvets, with their hair adorned with jewels.

For Money, Not Love

In 15th-century Florence, as in much of Italy, girls married as young as 14. Well-born men, it was expected, would have had several lovers, and possibly **illegitimate** children, before they decided to take a wife. The process of choosing just the right wife was generally left to the nobleman's family. Marriage was a way of gaining political power and social status; love was a secondary consideration. In order to ensure an advantageous marriage, the family of the bride-to-be was expected to pay the groom's family a dowry. A dowry was an amount of money or goods given, in effect, to "buy" the groom. This could include the bride's **trousseau**: a collection of expensive clothes, fine linen, and jewelry bought over many years in preparation for her role as a wife.

A wife's chief role was to produce male children. These she would raise with the help of her mother-in-law. According to custom, the groom's mother took an active role in choosing her son's wife, nursemaids for the children, and staff for the house. A noblewoman's status depended entirely on good marriage connections and how many healthy sons she produced.

On the birth of a male child, birth trays were often made to celebrate the event. These showed the birth scene, with the mother and richly dressed female family members in attendance on the newborn infant. (Birth trays were not made if the newborn was a girl.) Newborns were wrapped in strips of plain or embroidered cloth called swaddling clothes.

Keeping Young and Beautiful

Venetian women went to elaborate lengths to maintain their skin's youthful appearance. Early face masks and moisturizers included raw veal, which was laid in strips across the skin, and animal dung, which was rubbed liberally all over the body and face.

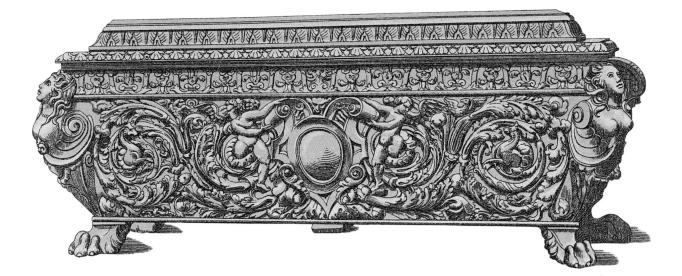

This gilded chest, called a *cassone*, was designed to hold a bride's trousseau, which might include clothing, household linen, and jewels. *Cassones* could be up to eight feet (2.4 m) long and were used throughout the Renaissance period.

Occasionally, women who had reached their twenties without finding a suitable husband entered a convent to find a useful life—the only alternative to marriage for the daughter of a rich family.

The Renaissance Ideal

During the Renaissance, beauty was considered to be a sign of moral superiority. For women, outer beauty was seen as an indication of an inner spiritual perfection. Pale skin, a small mouth, high forehead, a long elegant neck, and a head of thick (preferably golden) curls were seen as ideal. Wealthy women who did not naturally have these attributes used every lotion, powder, and dye they could find to attain them.

Blond was a particularly popular hair color for women, but achieving the required shade was a long process. First, the dye had to be prepared. Alum, black sulfur, and honey were combined in the following proportions: six pounds (2.72 kg) of alum, six ounces (170 g) of sulfur, and four ounces (115 g)

The Sweet Smell of Success

Rouge, face powders, nail polish, and perfume were used in large quantities by Italian noblewomen. During the 16th century, if people washed at all, they used cold water, which, in unheated homes, could easily bring on colds and fevers. With medicine primitive at best, influenza (flu) was often a killer. It was considered better to cover up body odors with perfume than risk ill health by bathing too often.

For many women, convent life was the only respectable alternative to marriage. These figures are wearing typical convent dress from the 1600s: an Ursuline nun (left), a nun of the order of Saint Catherine with an orphan (center), and a nun from a nursing order (right).

of honey. This was mixed with water to make a thick paste that was applied to the hair. The hair was then spread out over the brim of a wide, crownless hat and allowed to dry in the sun. Thomas Coryat, an English traveler, was particularly amazed at the sight of women dyeing their hair on the roofs and balconies of Venice. Once the color was fixed in the sun, the desired golden locks could then be twisted into ringlets and curls using heated curling tongs, what Coryat called "a frisling or crisping pinne of iron."

Feminine Beauty

While rich Italian men of the Renaissance dressed to show off their figures, women, too, benefited from the revival of humanist ideas. Costumes for women between 1250 and 1350 had been generally long and loose-fitting, hiding the figure. But from 1360, women's clothes became more feminine and were cut to show off the figure.

By the mid-1400s, a long overgown called a *cioppa* was worn, with wide sleeves and a train of material that fell to the floor in folds. An undergown of a darker color was also usually worn, with the front of the overgown split or pinned up to

Wigs and Powder

During the 18th century, fashionable Italian men and women wore long wigs, powdered and curled in a style adopted from the French court. Wearing wigs required the natural hair to be shaved off entirely, or at least trimmed close to the head. By 1750, this was such an accepted part of fashionable attire that an unwigged applicant for an official post on the Venetian council was told: "We want a serious and responsible man to fill the post...and we shall not find him among...persons who wear their own hair." Women's wigs were often built into such tall, elaborate structures that Padua's professor of meteorology, Giuseppe Toaldo, suggested that women of style should be fitted with lightning conductors.

This image, based on Vecellio's painting of 1589, shows a Venetian woman dyeing her hair. Italian men also dyed their hair, although black, not blond, was the fashionable color.

show the contrast in the two garments. The upper part of the gown, the bodice, was tailored at the waist and bust, with a low neckline in a style called **décolleté**. A girdle was worn on the hips to further emphasize the female body shape.

Unlike their counterparts in the rest of Western Europe, who wore heavy and elaborate headdresses in the shape of horns or cones, most Italian women kept their heads bare. Hair was worn loose if unmarried, braided if married. Veils, popular in Venice, were worn far back on the head, with ribbons or strings of pearls wrapped around the hair for decoration.

Spanish Style

For the wealthy, Renaissance clothing was particularly rich, with heavy velvets and silks dyed in striking shades of red, brown, and green. For most of the Renaissance period, Italy influenced the fashions in the rest of Europe, but slowly, Italian fashions began to echo styles from other parts of the world. In Venice and the eastern states, for example, styles tended to have a more **Oriental** look, and the turban became popular with Italian women around 1450.

After 1519, when Charles I of Spain took over the rule of the Holy Roman Empire, Spanish fashions influenced the city-states of Milan, Florence, and Naples. The colonization of the Americas during the 16th century brought further wealth to the Spanish and Portuguese courts, and until the 1600s, these two nations dominated mainland Europe. With this newly acquired political power, Spanish costume spread to much of Catholic Europe.

Spanish fashion introduced a number of changes to the typical Italian Renaissance costume. The first of these was the addition of a high-necked collar with a **ruff** around the neck. This replaced the low-cut décolleté neckline around 1550. Spanish costume also introduced the first true corset and the hooped whalebone **farthingale**, which was worn by women around the waist to give the skirt a bell-like shape. Previously, gowns had followed the natural lines of the body. Catherine de' Medici, daughter of Florence's ruling family and queen of France, is credited with being the first to introduce this new style and make it popular in Italy.

A selection of popular headwear from the 15th century, as worn by Italian noblewomen. A diadem, shown upper left, was a popular style. A diadem was a band or chain worn around the head, usually decorated with a single hanging jewel.

Modesty and Lace

Spain was much more conservative than Italy. With the support of the Church, Spanish costume became increasingly plain, favoring heavy, unadorned black material. By the 1600s, clothing styles in much of the rest of Europe was more restrained. While still tightly tailored, clothes were now used to cover up rather than display the body. One exception was in sleeve length. For the first time since ancient Rome, three-quarter-length sleeves were fashionable. In Italy, ladies took advantage of this new style to wear tiny brocade muffs. Lace, a new material, was used for ruffs and for decoration around the cuffs of the sleeves.

Ruffs worn during the 16th century came in a variety of styles, and were sometimes worn in combination with a low-cut décolleté neckline.

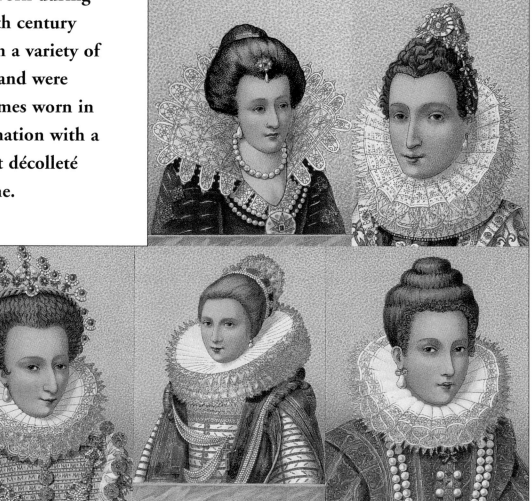

Lace can be made from most fine threads, including linen, cotton, silk, gold, and silver. Until the 19th century, lace was made by hand and often named after its place of manufacture. During the 1600s, Venetian lace was particularly sought after. Even today, *point de Venise*, which is a type of needlepoint lace made in a floral design, is still famed for its beauty.

But not all city-states adopted these new Spanish styles. Until the 1750s, many Italian fashions continued to reflect the independent nature of the city-states. Fynes Moryson, a traveler writing in 1617, noted the differences in costume throughout the region. While ladies in Genoa favored black velvet, Venetians still preferred lighter colors and richer materials. While some city-states were happy to adopt the corset and ruff, many simply took what they liked of the new styles and ignored the rest. Ruffs, for example, were sometimes combined with a low-cut décolleté neckline, with thin layers of gauze or lace covering the exposed upper chest. Similarly, layers of skirts, one on top of the other, were worn to give a fuller shape to the skirt, in place of the unwieldy farthingale. Venice, in particular, remained a law unto itself in the world of fashion.

Dieting Tip?

As lace grew in popularity, neck ruffs grew larger and larger. As many as five lace collars could be worn around the neck at once. These were kept tilted at the desired angle by being stiffened with wire. Some ruffs were so large that eating became difficult. Knives and forks were made with extra-long handles to ensure that diners could actually get the food to their mouths.

Venetian Excess

Despite strict sumptuary laws, Venetian fashions were probably the most extravagant and outlandish of all Italy's city-states.

Writing in the 17th century, traveler and author Fynes Moryson reported to his shocked readers that some Venetian noblewomen "shew their naked necks and brests." In Venice, the cut of the dress was so low that it barely covered the nipples. Just in case such a subtle sexual signal was missed, powder and rouge were applied over the breasts in red patches for emphasis.

Venetian fashion was also famous for the stiltlike shoes, called *zoccoli*, that noblewomen wore. Designed to prevent expensive dresses from being dragged through the mud, *zoccoli* had leather-covered wooden platform heels as much as 12 inches (30 cm) high. Most noblewomen had to rely on the assistance of their maids to be able to walk without injury. Thomas Coryat, an English traveler, saw one lady take a serious fall while attempting to walk without help. Rather than help the injured lady, Thomas considered her fall just desserts for wearing "such frivolous…ridiculous instruments." He was equally amused to see "what dwarfes they appear, when taken down from their wooden scaffolds."

Breaking the Law

Venetian women found many inventive ways around the sumptuary laws. After the Venetian government banned gold and silver cloth in 1443, women continued to wear it beneath other, plainer garments. Sleeves would then be cut in a style called slashing in order to show the richer, more expensive cloth below. Slashing was eventually banned—but it took 30 years for the law to catch up with the inventiveness of the lawbreakers. It was also common to use the letter of the law to avoid conforming to its intention. A woman found wearing banned buttons, for example, could claim that they were actually studs, as long as the garment had no buttonholes.

Hidden beneath their dresses, 16th-century Venetian women wore high-heeled shoes called *zoccoli*, which were usually brightly painted or gilded with gold leaf.

Ladies or Whores?

Within Venetian society, one group of women occupied a unique position. Neither wives nor mothers, courtesans had greater freedoms than most women of the period. A courtesan could be many things. She could be a successful high-class prostitute with a different lover every night. She could be the mistress of just one nobleman, who would keep her housed and dressed in luxury. She may even have had clients with whom she did not have a sexual relationship. Courtesans were not exactly socially acceptable in Venetian high society, but they were seen as necessary. In a culture where women were expected to be virgins on their wedding day, but men were allowed to have many lovers, courtesans provided the natural solution to such double standards. Despite the dubious way that they earned their living, many courtesans were extremely successful and well known.

These images show Italian costumes from the end of the 1500s: (left to right) a noblewoman, bride, widow, and merchant's wife. The figure on the far left wears a hooped skirt, which was fashionable in Milan. The other women are from Venice, where layering was often used to create a fuller shape.

As they spent much of their time in the company of the rich, courtesans were expected to be well-educated and well-dressed. Most courtesans dressed extravagantly, often setting fashions that the nobility later followed. In fact, many Venetians complained that it was impossible to tell a "lady" from a "whore." To combat this, sumptuary laws were enacted to prevent courtesans from wearing gold, silver, pearl necklaces, earrings, or silk. *Flora*, a famous painting by the Venetian artist Tintoretto (1518–1594), was painted between 1570 and 1580. It shows the courtesan Veronica Franco wearing a rich crimson gown and tight-fitting silk bodice. Around her neck is a string of pearls, and on her ears she wears a pair of exquisite hooped gold earrings. A similar painting, called *Courtesan Playing Lute* (ca. 1550–1570) shows another courtesan, also wearing silk and pearls. It may have been that both women chose to dress in this way in an attempt to look like "an honest woman." However, it is more probable that, like many other Venetians, they simply chose to ignore the sumptuary laws.

Horatio Brown (1854–1926), an author who lived in Venice from 1879, believed that, for Venetians, culture and tradition were tightly bound up with costume. To be truly Venetian, he said, one had to be well-dressed.

Wearing Underwear

Little is known about early Renaissance women's underwear, but it is believed that the Duchess of Ferrara, illegitimate daughter of Pope Alexander VI, may have brought the idea to Italy from Spain. Fynes Moryson, writing in the 17th century, declared that in Venice "virgins, and especially gentlewomen...wear silke or linen breeches under their gowns." Courtesans often wore male-style clothing as undergarments. These were sometimes embroidered with saucy or romantic sayings, such as "I want the heart."

Switzerland and the Tirol

Like Italy, the Swiss nation began life as a collection of small, fiercely independent states. Today these states, called cantons, retain many of their traditions and modes of dress.

Switzerland is a small country nestled on a plateau between the Jura and the Alpine mountain ranges. Sandwiched between Italy, Austria, France, and Germany, Swiss culture echoes many of the traditions of its neighbors. Modern Switzerland has three official languages—German, French, and Italian—and a population that is split 50/50 between Catholics and Protestants. A fourth unofficial language, Romansh, is similar to Latin, which was the language of the ancient Roman and much of the Holy Roman Empire for centuries.

Welcome to Helvetia

Helvetia is the Latin name for Switzerland. The Romans gave this name to the region after the Celtic tribe, the Helvetians, who lived in the area. The

The man in the center wears the traditional costume of Unterwangenberg. The others are both from the Brixen (Bressanone) Valley. The breeches worn by the men, and the gathered skirt and apron worn by the woman, are common to many of the region's folk costumes.

Helvetians were conquered by the Roman Empire around 58 B.C. The name Helvetia is still used today by the Swiss on their coins and postage stamps.

While, centuries after the fall of Rome, Italian culture continued to look back to ancient Roman ideas and traditions for guidance, Switzerland's main cultural influences were German. After the fall of Rome, Germanic tribes occupied much of what would become modern-day Switzerland. In A.D. 962, Switzerland came under the control of the Holy Roman Empire, which was also dominated by powerful Austrian and Germanic nobles until the 1500s.

In 1291, three Swiss regions—Schwyz, Uri, and Unterwalden—decided to establish themselves as an independent nation. They agreed to help each other fight against foreign rule and invited other states to sign a Perpetual Covenant. This was the start of the "Swiss Confederation." The Swiss **cantons** won complete independence in 1499, but it took the Holy Roman Empire until 1648 to officially recognize them as a nation.

In many ways, however, the cantons remained independent states. Even by the beginning of the 20th century, Switzerland could not really be seen as one nation, but many. Local patriotism remained strong, and each canton was noticeably different from its neighbor. Today, there are 23 cantons, and these still show many regional differences. In culture, language, religion, and national costume, each canton remains unique.

This woman is dressed in the traditional costume from Emmental and Plateau, in the canton of Bern. The laced bodice was particularly popular in the German-speaking cantons (or states).

Germany, Austria, and the Tirol

Swiss regional costume, still worn for modern-day festivals, varies widely from canton to canton. Just as in the Italian city-states, each region had its own definite styles—some uniquely Swiss, some showing the influence of other nations.

Costumes from German-speaking cantons, for example, tended to have one dominant color. Women wore skirts of rich dark brown, blue, or black. In Bern, women wore a bodice, usually red on the back and sides, with a yellow panel on the front, whose lacing was wound around small silver buttons. During the 17th and 18th centuries, Switzerland was famous for its embroidery, and such bodices are fine examples of some of the most beautiful Swiss needlework. Over the plain-colored skirt, a brightly patterned pink-, blue-, or green-striped apron was traditionally worn.

This style of dress was similar to the national costumes of the Tirol. The Tirol is a semi-independent mountainous region on Switzerland's border, which is split geographically into a southern area, governed by Italy, and a

The bride (left) is from the Fribourg canton. Although this image is from the 19th century, the clothes are from an earlier generation, showing the tradition of brides wearing their grandmother's clothing on their wedding day.

Something Old...

It used to be a popular custom in Switzerland for couples who were getting married to wear their grandparents' clothing on their wedding day. This is why some of the paintings from the 19th century show young couples wearing clothes that are as much as 100 years out of date. Luckily, perhaps, for modern brides and grooms, there are few people who still observe this tradition today.

northern area, ruled by Austria. The national costume of Tirolean women is called a *dirndl*. This includes a blouse, a lace-up bodice, a skirt, and a brightly decorated apron. The Tirol, like Switzerland, was ruled first by the Romans, then by Germanic tribes, and finally by the Holy Roman Empire. It is not surprising, then, with similar cultural influences and such a geographical closeness, that national costumes in the German-speaking Swiss cantons are similar to those in the Tirol.

Cantons and Costumes

This variation in national costume from region to region extended throughout Switzerland. In the southern cantons, national costumes showed an Italian love of bright color and elaborate floral designs. In contrast, national costumes from the cantons that border France favored pastel shades. Plain skirts with pastel-striped aprons were worn, and small lace shawls completed the effect. In most cantons, shirt sleeves for women were worn three-quarter length. This allowed the addition of elegant, elbow-length black lace gloves in western regions.

It was in the Romansh-speaking cantons bordering Austria that the greatest regional variations in costume were seen. Women's skirts were pleated rather than allowed to follow the natural line of the body, which was the fashion in the rest of Switzerland. Colors, too, were more subdued. In Haute-Engadine,

Traditional 19th-century Swiss costumes. On the left, a young girl from Lucerne, wearing an embroidered bodice, a straw bonnet, and a checked knee-length apron over a plainer skirt.

in the Grisons canton, a long-sleeved, black-velvet bodice, apron, and cap were worn. These were all delicately embroidered with gold thread, which, against the lush, dark tones of the velvet, made a stunning visual effect.

The Reformation

Switzerland's long association with Germany has given Swiss costume through the ages a distinctly Germanic appearance. However, it was the Reformation that had the greatest impact on Swiss art and ideas, which were ultimately reflected in its costume. While the humanistic ideals of the Renaissance were particularly influential on southern European costume, northern European dress tended to reflect the ideas of the Reformation. In England, Germany, Holland, and Switzerland, the Reformation had almost exactly the opposite effect of the Renaissance on how people dressed.

The Reformation was a religious movement that was born out of protest against the wealth and abuses in the Church. Over the centuries, the Church had grown in size and influence. By the 1500s, many people were beginning to be scandalized by the great wealth of the Papacy and the abuse of power by many of its leading clerics. The growing protest against the Church ultimately gave birth to the Protestant churches. Protestants continued to follow the main

These two women are from the canton of Fribourg. The long aprons are held up to show the rich red gown beneath. The necklace worn by both women is a traditional silver medallion called an Agnus Dei.

beliefs of the Christian faith, but rejected, among other things, the rule of the Pope in Rome. In Switzerland, Huldreich Zwingli and John Calvin led the reform movement. In Germany, it was Martin Luther.

Protestants believed in the need for simplicity, restraint, decency, and hard work. This had a shattering impact on most countries of Europe, causing political and religious upheavals as Protestants and Catholics fought for control. It also had a great impact on costume, as Protestants favored a simpler, more serious form of dress. Costume in many parts of Switzerland—especially Geneva, which was John Calvin's center of Protestant power—was therefore more subdued than in southern Europe. Because of the Reformation, the fashion excesses seen in Italy's city-states would never be repeated in the Swiss cantons.

Military Dress

The enemy infantry advanced slowly, spear tips gleaming in the clear morning light. Before them, much of the Swiss army had already broken and soldiers

Clothing in the more mountainous regions of Switzerland, such as Bern, tended to be shorter. This was a practical consideration, making walking up steep mountain paths much easier.

were running back toward their own lines, dropping their swords and lances as they ran. Suddenly, from the confused ranks, rushed one lone figure. With a booming battle cry, he rushed at the advancing spearmen. Grabbing as many of the deadly spear points as he could in his bare hands, the lone soldier threw himself onto his enemy's weapons. Behind him, his comrades saw their chance. In their rush to tackle this one crazed Swiss man, the Austrians had left a hole in their own defensive lines. With a cheer, the Swiss rushed toward the gap, pushing their enemy back in confusion.

This story of Arnold von Winkerlried tells the legend of one of Switzerland's most famous national heroes. Arnold supposedly fought during Switzerland's struggles for independence from the Holy Roman Empire in the 13th and 14th centuries. Throughout its history, Switzerland has been famous for the bravery of its soldiers.

Foreign nations often hired Swiss mercenaries to help them win wars, which brought in much-needed money to the regions. Swiss mercenaries were often

Going to Great Lengths

In the 19th century, women from Bern grew their hair to extraordinary lengths, sometimes down to their ankles. Once they were married, this hair would be gathered into two long braids that were then coiled on top of the head.

recognizable on the battlefields because of the bright colors they wore—soldiers from each canton being dressed in the colors of their own region.

The Swiss Guard

After 1874, the Swiss constitution banned all Swiss men from fighting for foreign powers. The only exception to this rule was the Swiss Guard. The Swiss Guard, founded by Pope Julius II in 1505, are the Pope's personal bodyguards. Originally, Swiss mercenaries were hired by the Pope because of their reputation for bravery and honesty. There are currently 107 men in the Swiss Guard, including five officers and a chaplain. All members of the Swiss Guard (also called the *Cohors Helvetica*) are recruited from volunteers from Switzerland's Roman Catholic cantons. In the past, all potential applicants had to be German-speaking, but now French- and Italian-speaking men can also apply.

Like the French Foreign Legion and the British Army's Gurkhas, the Swiss Guard is unusual in that its soldiers are employed by a state that is not their own. Every year, on May 6, the soldiers of the Swiss Guard kneel before the Pope and swear to serve him "to the death." That date is the anniversary of the invasion of Rome in 1527 by the army of Charles V of Spain (called the Sack of Rome). On that day, 147 Swiss soldiers died defending the Pope, and from then on, Swiss soldiers were chosen in preference to those from any other nation.

The clothes of this young Swiss woman from the Schwyz canton, are typical of 18th-century costume, particularly the tall fan-like headdress and long silk gown.

The appearance of the Swiss Guard is rather striking. There are strict regulations on their age and height. A man must be between 18 and 25 years old and at least 5 feet 8 inches (1.7 m) tall. It is also rumored that the men are expected to be good-looking, although there is no official written regulation that states this.

Lined up in St. Peter's Square in the center of Vatican City, the Swiss Guard adds a dash of style and pomp. Originally, the Guard wore the standard military uniform of the day. In 1548, the uniform was adopted that is still worn to this day. It is commonly believed that this uniform was designed by Michelangelo (1475–1564), although no historical evidence exists to support this. Nevertheless, the appearance of the Swiss Guard is unforgettable. Dressed in bright yellow, red, and blue Renaissance dress, the soldiers are living reminders of the long and rich histories of both Switzerland and Italy.

Cut, Thrust, and Slash

Swiss pikemen were particularly famous for their skill in holding back cavalry charges. They were also responsible for popularizing one of the 16th century's most striking fashions—slashing. Slashing involved cutting the outer garment, generally on the sleeves. The richer material worn below would then be pulled through the cuts.

Slashing was a popular fashion with both men and women between 1520 and 1540. It was believed to have developed from a style of costume worn by Swiss mercenaries, who were called lansquenets. There are many tales of how Swiss mercenaries came to wear slashed clothing. In one, the mercenaries used their defeated enemy's flags to mend their torn uniforms, sewing the multicolored flag silk to the inside of their torn tunics and thus creating the slashed effect. Another, less glamorous tale tells how they tore their own uniforms—revealing the material beneath—in order to make them more comfortable to wear on the battlefield.

Glossary

Note: Specialized words relating to clothing are explained within the text, but those that appear more than once are listed below for easy reference.

Brocade generally silk fabric with a raised pattern

Canton one of the small states that make up the Swiss confederation

Centurion officer in charge of a unit of 100 Roman soldiers

Chiton basic Greek robe worn long or short

Couplet two lines of rhyming verse

Damask reversible silk or linen fabric with a woven pattern

Décolleté low-cut neckline

Doge the chief magistrate in Venice or Genoa

Ermine white, winter fur of the weasel-like animal of the same name

Etiquette correct behavior

Farthingale whalebone rings worn around the waist to give a skirt a bell shape

Faux pas a French phrase meaning an awkward mistake, especially socially

Fleur-de-lis often used in heraldry, this is a design of a lily with three petals

Fresco painting done on wet plaster

Gauls tribe occupying much of France and Belgium, conquered by Rome (around 100–51 B.C.)

Girdle belt or sash

Hellenization to become like the Greeks

Himation long, woolen Greek cloak worn draped around the body

Hose type of stocking

Illegitimate when referring to a child, it means he or she was born to parents who are not married to each other

Licentious indulging in casual sexual activity

Middle Ages period from the fall of Rome to the start of the Renaissance

Mummy ancient Egyptian preserved body wrapped in linen strips

Nap a downy or hairy surface on cloth

Opulence ostentatious wealth

Oriental eastern

Papacy the government of the Catholic Church with the Pope as the supreme head

Posterity future generations

Pourpoint man's padded and quilted tunic or doublet with a short, above-the-knee skirt

Prowess superior skill

Pumice stone volcanic rock used for smoothing rough surfaces

Punic Wars three Roman wars (264–146 B.C.) against the Carthaginian empire in North Africa; victorious Rome leveled Carthage and sowed the site with salt

Renaissance "rebirth" of the ideas of classical Rome and Greece that began in Italy (ca. 1300–1600).

Ruff circle of lace worn around the neck

Samite heavy silk

Samnites tribe from the mountains south of Rome

Satirist someone who uses humor to point out society's faults

Stola long, flowing garment worn by Roman women.

Sumptuary laws laws restricting extravagant expenditure on, and choice of, clothes, especially to define social classes

Toga man's draped robe that could only be worn by Roman citizens

Trousseau a girl's possessions collected in preparation for married life, such as clothing, linen, and household items

Tunica Roman tunic, similar to a Greek chiton, worn indoors

Tyrian purple expensive dye made from crushed whelk shells

Vestments priestly clothing used for ceremonies

Zoccoli stilt-like shoes worn by Venetian women

Timeline

800 B.C.	Etruscans arrive on the Italian peninsula.
753	Legendary founding of Rome by Romulus and Remus.
600	Etruscans conquer Latinum.
509	Rome drives out the Etruscan kings; the Republic of Rome is established.
58	Roman republic conquers Helvetia (Switzerland).
27	Rome becomes an empire under its first emperor, Augustus.
15	Roman Empire conquers the Tirol.
A.D. 395	Roman Empire is split into eastern and western territories; the eastern part becomes the Byzantine empire.
476	Odoacer overthrows the last Roman emperor.
800	Charlemagne is crowned King of Rome.
962	Start of the Holy Roman Empire; German and Austrian nobles rule as Holy Roman Emperors for almost 500 years.
1291	Three Swiss cantons establish a Swiss Confederation and fight for independence from the Holy Roman Empire.
1350	Start of the Renaissance in Italy.
1453	Ottoman Turks conquer the Byzantine empire.
1519	Charles I of Spain becomes Holy Roman Emperor and brings a Spanish feel to much of European art and costume.
1648	The Swiss nation is recognized by the Holy Roman Empire.
1861	Kingdom of Italy is founded under the rule of King Victor Emmanuel II.
1871	Rome becomes Italy's capital.
1914–1918	World War I; the Tirol is split between Italy and Austria.
1939–1945	World War II; Italy enters the war in 1940; Switzerland, following a centuries-long tradition, remains neutral.
1946	Republic of Italy is established.

Online Sources

A Brief History of Fashion
www.furman.edu/~kgossman/history/index
An excellent site with a wide range of
information for students of all ages.

The Costumer's Manifesto
www.costumes.org/
A great starting point for further research. This
site offers a wide range of information and links
on costume throughout the ages. Of particular
interest are the following pages:
www.costumes.org/pages/timelinepages/
   ancientrome
www.costumes.org/pages/fashiondress/
   latemedieval
www. costumes.org/pages/renports

Courtesans in Venice
http://virtualpark.uga.edu/cdesmet/jason/court.htm
An interesting article that is a good starting point
for research into what can be a complex subject.

Early Renaissance Fashion Terms
http://www.furman.edu/~kgossman/history/ear
lyren/terms.htm
Part of the "Brief History of Fashion" site, these
excellent pages give clear, concise definitions of
Renaissance fashion terms. Images, links, and a
timeline provide additional clarification.

Virtual Rome
http://www.vroma.org
A good site for students and teachers, with
information on all aspects of life in ancient Rome.

Further Reading

Barrow, Reginald Haynes. *The Romans.* London:
Penguin, 1985.

Goodenough, Simon. *Citizens of Rome.* London:
Hamlyn, 1979.

Hearder, Harry. *Italy: A Short History.*
Cambridge: C.U.P, 1996.

Hibbert, Christopher. *Venice: The Biography of a
City.* London: Grafton, 1988.

Kitto, Humphrey David. *The Greeks.* London:
Penguin, 1985.

Latham, Ronald. *The Travels of Marco Polo.*
London: Folio Society, 1997.

Power, Eileen. *Medieval People.* London: Folio
Society, 1999.

Scott, Jack Cassin. *Costumes and Settings for
Historical Plays. Vol. 2, The Medieval Period.*
London: Batsford, 1979.

Settembrini, Luigi. *1951–2001: Made in Italy?*
Milan: Skira, 2002.

Stibbert, Frederic. *European Civil and Military
Clothing: From the First to the Eighteenth
Century.* Mineola, NY: Dover, 2001.

Vance, Peggy. *Illustrated History of European
Costume: Period Styles and Accessories.* London:
Collins and Brown, 2000.

About the Author

Paula Hammond was born and educated in the
ancient Roman town of Chester, England. After
completing a degree in History, Literature, and
Theology at Trinity College, she moved to
London to pursue a career in publishing. Her
writing credits include *Communication Through*
The Ages, which traces the history of writing
and communication, and *The Grubbiest
Adventure...Ever*, a project-based research
resource for young children. She is currently
writing a series for teenagers on notable
historical figures and events.

Index